Quick Study ACADEMIC — English Fundamentals 1 — Grammar · Parts of Speech

Boost confidence & test scores!

What Is Grammar?

Grammar is a **set of rules** on how to put **words**, **phrases**, and **clauses** together to **express ideas** clearly. It describes the various kinds of words and their uses in a sentence.

PARTS OF SPEECH

Words are classified into the following **parts of speech**: noun, pronoun, adjective, verb, adverb, preposition, conjunction, and interjection. Many words can belong to more than one part of speech, depending on how they are used. For example, the word "back" can be used as a noun, an adjective, and a verb.

EX:
My **back** is aching! (noun)
He entered through the **back** door. (adjective)
Both candidates said they would **back** the bill. (verb)

Abbreviations

noun	n.	preposition	prep.
pronoun	p.	conjunction	conj.
adjective	adj.	interjection	interj.
verb	v.	singular	sing.
adverb	adv.	plural	pl.

NOUNS

FUNCTION: name people, places, things, or ideas.
TYPES:
PROPER nouns name **specific** people, places, or things, and always begin with a capital letter.
COMMON nouns name **non-specific** people, places, or things and are not capitalized unless they begin a sentence.

EX:

PROPER nouns	COMMON nouns
J.R.R. Tolkien	author
Philadelphia	city
Statue of Liberty	monument

ABSTRACT nouns refer to states, concepts, feelings, or qualities, and **CONCRETE nouns** refer to tangible things that can be perceived through the senses.

EX:

ABSTRACT nouns	CONCRETE nouns
loneliness	star
equality	flag
joy	ice cream
beauty	song

COUNT nouns name things that can be expressed in plural form, usually with an **-s**, such as "dog/dogs," "hat/hats," "plate/plates," and "teacher/teachers." **NON-COUNT nouns**, also known as **MASS nouns**, refer to things that usually cannot be counted, such as "flour," "weather," "milk," and "thunder." Non-count nouns are always considered singular and take a singular verb.

n. sing.   v. sing.
EX: The lightning lights up the night sky.

COLLECTIVE nouns refer to groups of people or things, such as "team," "audience," "class," "committee," and "jury." They are usually singular unless it is clear that the members within the group are acting as individuals, as indicated in the second example.

n. sing.   v. sing.
EX: A colony of bees lives in my garden.

n. pl.   v. pl.
The jury disagree on the guilt of the accused.

PLURAL nouns indicate more than one, and most form the plural by adding **-s**.
EX:

boy	→	boys
town	→	towns
table	→	tables

Nouns ending in **s**, **sh**, **ch**, or **x** form the plural by adding **-es**.
EX:

bus	→	buses
bush	→	bushes
church	→	churches
box	→	boxes

Most nouns ending in **f** drop the **f** and add **-ves**.
EX:

loaf	→	loaves
wharf	→	wharves

Nouns ending in a **consonant + y** drop the **y** and add **-ies**.
EX:

baby	→	babies
sky	→	skies

Nouns ending in an **o** preceded by a vowel add **-s**.
EX:

video	→	videos
stereo	→	stereos

Nouns ending in an **o** preceded by a consonant add **-es**.
EX:

hero	→	heroes
potato	→	potatoes

HYPHENATED COMPOUNDS add **-s** to the main word.
EX:

brother-in-law	→	brothers-in-law
maid-of-honor	→	maids-of-honor

Several nouns have **irregular plural forms**. These can be found in a dictionary.
EX:

child	→	children
woman	→	women
mouse	→	mice
goose	→	geese

Some nouns keep their **Latin** or **Greek form** in the plural. These can also be found in a dictionary.
EX:

nucleus	→	nuclei
fungus	→	fungi
crisis	→	crises
criterion	→	criteria

Nouns can have different **functions** in a sentence: **subject, direct object, indirect object, object of a preposition**.

EX:
John is my best friend. (subject)
I saw that movie. (direct object)
We bought Eva an ice cream. (indirect object)
My friends went to the mall. (object of preposition)

POSSESSIVE nouns express **ownership** of a noun previously mentioned, known as an **antecedent**. Most possessive nouns are formed by adding **'s**.

EX:
That jacket? It's John's.
(The jacket belongs to John.)
Those toys? They're the children's.
(The toys belong to the children.)
This pen? It's James's.
(The pen belongs to James.)

PLURAL nouns that end in **s** just add an apostrophe to become possessive.

EX:
Whose soccer ball? It's the boys'.
(The soccer ball belongs to the boys.)
Whose books? They're the students'.
(The books belong to the students.)

POSSESSIVE nouns can also be used as adjectives and are formed in the same way, by adding **'s** or simply an apostrophe, depending on whether the noun is singular or plural.

EX:
It's Harry's car.
(The car belongs to Harry.)
The singers' voices are highly trained.
(The voices belong to the singers.)

APPOSITIVES are noun phrases that can come before or after other nouns or pronouns to explain or describe them.

EX:
A miniature black poodle, Tony's dog is very cuddly.
Margie, my sister, is on the varsity basketball team.

VERBS (continued)

The **progressive tenses** indicate ongoing action in the present, past, or future.

TRANSITIVE verbs take a **direct object**. Asking "whom" or "what" after a verb will let you know whether or not a verb is transitive.

EX: She made a cake. (made what? *a cake*)
Anna saw them last week at the movies. (saw whom? *them*)

INTRANSITIVE verbs have **no direct object**. The verb may express action, but the action is not done to anyone or anything.

EX: We slept late on Saturday. (slept whom or what?)
They stood in line for an hour. (stood whom or what?)

VERB FORMS (VERBALS):
INFINITIVES (base word + "to") can be used as a **noun** or an **adjective**.

EX: To love is important. (noun, subject of the verb "is")
Jen wants to sing. (noun, object of the verb "wants")
Lori has stories to tell. (adjective, modifies "stories")

PARTICIPLES (base verb + suffix) can be used as **adjectives** to modify nouns or pronouns. Like infinitives and gerunds, participles are based on verbs and express action or a state of being. Present participles end in **-ing**. Past participles end in **-ed**, **-en**, **-d**, **-t**, or **-n**.

EX: The singing canary flew out the window. (present)
Exhausted, she went to bed to take a nap. (past)
The frozen man sat by the fire to warm up. (past)

GERUNDS are **present participles** that are used in sentences as **nouns** and can be used in any way that a noun can—as a subject, object, or object of a preposition.

EX: Driving without a seatbelt can be dangerous. (subject)
I always like reading a good book at the beach. (object)
Max wrote an essay about the benefits of eating well. (object of preposition)

ADVERBS

FUNCTION: modify verbs, adjectives, or other adverbs.
TYPES:
When adverbs **modify verbs**, they answer questions such as "How?", "When?", "Where?", or "How often?". Many adverbs are easily recognized because they end with the suffix **-ly**.

EX: Jane spoke softly. (how)
Li went to the library yesterday. (when)
Paula left her bookbag here. (where)
It rains frequently in the country. (how often)

When adverbs **modify adjectives**, they always come before the adjectives they modify.

EX: That statement is entirely true.
It was a wonderfully quiet afternoon.

Adverbs that **modify other adverbs** are also known as **INTENSIFIERS** and always come before the adverb they modify.

EX: The baby cried quite loudly because she was hungry.
We stared rather intently at the painting.

CONJUNCTIVE adverbs are used to join two clauses together. A conjunctive adverb is often preceded by a semicolon and followed by a comma.

EX: I should have gone to bed; instead, I watched a movie.
It is raining; otherwise, I would have gone to the beach.

Conjunctive Adverbs

also	meanwhile
consequently	nevertheless
finally	next
furthermore	otherwise
however	still
indeed	then
instead	therefore
likewise	thus

PREPOSITIONS

FUNCTION: combine nouns or pronouns to create phrases that modify verbs, nouns, pronouns, or adjectives.

PREPOSITIONS and objects make up **prepositional phrases** that give details on time, space, and direction to help us better understand a sentence. **Prepositional phrases** can function as a **noun**, an **adjective**, or an **adverb**.

EX: She rummaged through the attic of her house looking for old treasures.

[NOTE: The first prepositional phrase functions as an adverb because it modifies the verb by describing where she rummaged. The second phrase modifies the noun "attic," which is the object of the first prepositional phrase, and describes which attic she rummaged through.]

Common Prepositions

about	from
above	in/inside/into
across	like
after	near
against	of
along	off
among	on/onto
around	out/outside
at	over
before	past
behind	since
below	through
beneath	throughout
beside	to
between	toward
beyond	under
by	underneath
down	until
during	up/upon
except	with/within
for	without

CONJUNCTIONS

FUNCTION: join words or groups of words in a sentence.
TYPES:
COORDINATING conjunctions connect words and clauses of equal status.

EX: We bought apples and bananas.
We saw many clouds, yet it didn't rain.

SUBORDINATING conjunctions join clauses of unequal status. In other words, one clause is dependent on the other.

EX: After Ted ran the marathon, he collapsed in exhaustion.
Linda didn't want to go to the mall because she didn't have any money.

CORRELATIVE conjunctions must join elements that are alike.

EX: I had to either study for the test or risk failing it.
Not only did she forget to bring the cake, but she also forgot to bake it!

Coordinating Conjunctions

and	or
but	so
for	yet
nor	

Common Subordinating Conjunctions

after	before	than	when
although	how	that	where
as	if	though	whether
because	since	until	while

Correlative Conjunctions

both…and
either…or
neither…nor
not only…but also
so…as
whether…or

INTERJECTIONS

FUNCTION: convey emotion in a sentence.
INTERJECTIONS often start a sentence but are not part of a sentence's actual grammar. Interjections often end with an **exclamation point**.

EX: Well, she said she'd be here at 8 o'clock.
Wow! That was some ri[de]

ISBN-13: 978-142320870-9
ISBN-10: 1423208706
©2009 BarCharts, Inc. 0810

Customer Hotline # 1.800.230.9522

T4-AZQ-996

PRONOUNS

FUNCTION: take the place of nouns.
TYPES:
PERSONAL pronouns refer to specific persons or things. Pronouns often refer back to their noun antecedent. Therefore, it is important to use them correctly so that your meaning is clear.

EX: When my friends got the news, they called me.

As each student arrives, she will take a seat.

The plural antecedent (friends) in the first sentence takes a plural pronoun (they). The singular antecedent (student) in the second sentence takes singular pronouns (he/she). The personal pronouns in both sentences above are called **SUBJECT** pronouns and function as the subject of the main verb.

Subject Pronouns

Singular	Plural
I	we
you	you
he/she/it	they

OBJECT pronouns are personal pronouns used as the object of a verb, preposition, or infinitive phrase, as in the examples below. Note how the object pronouns respectively refer back to their antecedent.

Object Pronouns

Singular	Plural
me	us
you	you
him/her/it	them

EX: The eagle? Did Meg really see it?

The children are bored; please give the toys to them.

Do you know Marsha? I was hoping to call her today.

POSSESSIVE pronouns are used to indicate ownership, as in, "Is the hat mine or yours?" Possessive pronouns can also be used as adjectives that modify nouns or noun phrases, as in, "The Lord of the Rings is his favorite movie." Possessive pronouns and adjectives can refer back to a noun and must agree with it in gender and number as in the following examples, respectively.

Possessive Pronouns/Adjectives

mine/my	ours/our
yours/your	yours/your
his, hers, its / his, her, its	theirs/their

EX: The twins decided not to wear theirs today.

Each student must turn in her report by Monday.

DEMONSTRATIVE pronouns point to or identify nouns. **This** and **these** refer to things that are nearby or close in time. **That** and **those** refer to things that are farther away or more distant in time. Demonstrative pronouns often function as **adjectives**.

EX: I have many hats, but this is my favorite.

adj.
That hat is exquisite!

adj.
These books are my all-time favorites.

adj.   p.
That pile of books? Those aren't very good at all!

Demonstrative Pronouns/Adjectives

Singular	Plural
this	these
that	those

REFLEXIVE pronouns **refer back to the subject** of a sentence or a clause and are used when the subject and the object of a verb or preposition are the same, and to emphasize the subject, as demonstrated in the following sentences, respectively.

EX: Dottie cut herself on the sharp knife.

They bought bagels for themselves.

I will do it myself.

Reflexive Pronouns

Singular	Plural
myself	ourselves
yourself	yourselves
herself	themselves
himself	themselves
itself	themselves

INTERROGATIVE pronouns are used to ask questions. **Who** acts as the subject of a verb and **whom** as the object of a verb or a preposition.

subject
EX: Who is knocking at the door?

object of prep.
To whom shall I give the flowers?

Interrogative Pronouns

who	whom
which	what

RELATIVE pronouns introduce **subordinate clauses** that function as adjectives and refer back to the noun or pronoun that the clause modifies. Like the interrogative pronoun **who** functions as the subject of a clause or sentence, and **whom** functions as the object of a verb or preposition.

subject of subordinate clause
EX: The girl who won the tennis match is my cousin.

object of prep.
These are the people for whom we are fighting.

Relative Pronouns

who	that
whom	which

INDEFINITE pronouns refer to **non-specific** persons or things. Most are always singular and take a singular verb. Some are always plural and take a plural verb. Some can also function as adjectives.

Indefinite Pronouns

all	anything	everything	one
another	both	many	several
any	each	nobody	some
anybody	everybody	none	somebody
anyone	everyone	no one	someone

p. sing.
EX: Does everyone have paper and a pencil?

p. pl.
Many have the means to get through difficult times.

adj. pl.
All books must be returned to the library by Saturday.

adj. sing.
Each member of the team will receive a trophy.

RECIPROCAL pronouns indicate a **mutual action** in which two or more people participate equally. When two people are involved, use **each other**. When more than two people are involved, use **one another**.

EX: The girls talk to each other every day after school.

The members of the team gave one another a high-five after winning the game.

RECIPROCAL pronouns can also be used as **possessive adjectives**.

EX: Sue and Mary borrowed each other's dresses.

The students read one another's reports.

> **quick tip!** Don't confuse possessive adjectives with contractions!
>
> **POSSESSIVE ADJECTIVE**   **CONTRACTION**
>
> its (*belonging to* it)   it's (short for "it is")
>
> your (*belonging to* you)   you're (short for "you are")
>
> their (*belonging to* them)   they're (short for "they are")
>
> whose (*belonging to* whom)   who's (short for "who is")

ADJECTIVES

FUNCTION: describe people or things in a sentence.
TYPES:
DESCRIPTIVE adjectives always come before the noun or noun phrase they modify and answer one of these questions: "Which one?", "What kind?", "How many?"

EX: The black hat is mine. (Which one?)
Long-stemmed roses are elegant. (What kind?)
There were 10 candles on the cake. (How many?)

PREDICATE adjectives follow linking verbs and describe the subject.

EX: Keisha is happy.
The books seem interesting.
Mark's help has been invaluable.

COMPARATIVE adjectives are used to **compare two** things. The suffix **-er** is used to form most comparatives. When a two-syllable adjective ends in **y**, **-ier** is used. Adjectives with three or more syllables are preceded by the word **more**.

EX: The Ohio River is longer than the Mississippi River.
Susan is happier than Paul.
Mark is more intelligent than Tim.

SUPERLATIVE adjectives are used to **compare three or more** things. The suffix **-est** is used to form most superlatives. When a two-syllable adjective ends in **y**, **-iest** is used. Adjectives with three or more syllables are preceded by the word **most**.

EX: The Missouri River is the longest river in the United States.
Debra is the happiest of all my friends.
Yuko is the most intelligent student of all.

Irregular Forms

Base	Comparative	Superlative
good	better	best
bad	worse	worst
little	less	least
much	more	most
far	farther/further	farthest/furthest

Some adjectives have **irregular comparative and superlative** forms. These need to be memorized.

PROPER adjectives come from **proper names** and are always capitalized.

EX: French bread
a Spanish omelet
the English countryside

VERBS

FUNCTION: express action or a state of being, and tell something about the subject.
TYPES:
MAIN, or **FINITE**, **verbs** change to match the form (number and person) of the subject or the tense of the verb (present, past, future, etc.). There are two types of main verbs: **ACTION verbs** and **LINKING verbs.**

• **ACTION** verbs express action that the subject carries out.

EX: Dan drove to his friend's house.

The horse jumped over the fence.

• **LINKING** verbs express a state of being and connect subjects to predicates, describing or renaming the subjects. Linking verbs include the "sense" verbs (to feel, to look, to taste, to smell). However, the most common linking verb is "to be."

EX: Carl and his brother are painters.

Mercedes seems happy today.

Common Linking Verbs

be	remain
feel	seem
grow	smell
look	taste

AUXILIARY verbs, also known as **HELPING verbs**, accompany main verbs to indicate tense, voice, mood, and number. Together, these verbs create **verb phrases**. In the following sentences, the auxiliary verbs are underlined and the main verbs are **bold**.

EX: I will **help** you wash the car today.
Has Mary **called** you yet about the report?
Arthur does **want** to go to the movies with you.

Auxiliary Verbs

be
have
do
can
may
will
shall
must

CHARACTERISTICS:
All finite verbs share five main characteristics: **NUMBER, PERSON, VOICE, MOOD** and **TENSE**. Finite verbs can also be **TRANSITIVE** or **INTRANSITIVE**.

NUMBER indicates how many things a verb refers to (singular–one; plural–more than one), and **PERSON** tells who or what does the action (first person—includes the self; second person–the person(s) spoken to; third person–the person(s) or thing(s) spoken about).

EX: I sit in silence listening to the birds. (first person singular)
You all have your books, correct? (second person plural)
Josh writes beautifully. (third person singular)

Active VOICE indicates that the subject of the sentence performs the action of the verb. **Passive VOICE** indicates that the subject receives the verb's action. Passive voice is easily recognized when the preposition "by" introduces the doer of the action.

EX: Mary wrote the book. (active)
The book was written by Mary. (passive)

MOOD indicates the manner in which an action or condition is expressed. The **indicative** mood expresses a statement, exclamation, or question. Verbs in the **subjunctive** mood express wishes, doubts, or statements that are contrary to fact. Verbs in the **imperative** mood make a demand or a request.

indicative
EX: What time is it? (question)

subjunctive
I wish you were here to see the show. (wish)

subjunctive
If he had been in charge, that would not have happened. (contrary to fact)

imperative
Please pass the salt. (request)

TENSE indicates the time of an action or condition. The basic verb tenses are present, past, and future.

The **perfect tenses** indicate that an action was completed at some time in the past, or will be completed at a specific time in the future.

TENSES	TIME	EXAMPLE
Present	present action/condition	He **writes** every day. We **are** happy today.
Past	completed action	I **watched** television last night.
Future	future action	I **will go** to the beach next summer.
PROGRESSIVE		
Present progressive	ongoing action	She **is eating** lunch right now.
Past progressive	past ongoing action interrupted by another action	I **was studying** when you called.
Future progressive	future ongoing action	I **will be sitting** in the park for the afternoon.
PERFECT		
Present perfect	action begun in the past and leading up to and including present	They **have seen** this movie twice.
Past perfect	action begun and completed in the past before another action occurred	Missy **had** already **left** the gym by the time I arrived.
Future perfect	action to be completed by or before a specific future time	By next week, my parents **will have sold** their house.
PERFECT/PROGRESSIVE		
Present perfect progressive	ongoing action begins in the past, continues in the present, and may continue into the future	I **have been cleaning** my room since Tuesday and I still haven't finished!
Past perfect progressive	ongoing past action completed before another action occurred	She **had been shopping** for two hours by the time we met for lunch.
Future perfect progressive	ongoing action begins in the past and continues to a specific future time	I **will have been writing** my paper for hours when the clock strikes 12!